WORKPACK
BONSAI

SUZAN SLATER

Andrews McMeel
Publishing

Kansas City

This edition published in 2004 by
Andrews McMeel Publishing
an Andrews McMeel Universal company
4520 Main Street
Kansas City, Missouri 64111.
First published in 2004
by Design Eye Publishing Ltd.

This book was conceived and produced by
Design Eye Publishing
Text by Suzan Slater
Designed by Elizabeth Healey
Edited by Joanna Smith

ISBN: 0-7407-4759-2

Manufactured in China

04 05 06 07 SDL 5 4 3 2 1

Contents

Introduction

Bonsai originated in China over 2,000 years ago, but it is the Japanese who have truly mastered the art since its introduction to Japan over 500 years ago. The word "bonsai" means a potted tree or planting in a tray. However, there is much more to bonsai than this— bonsai are living sculptures that are never truly finished but continue to grow and evolve as the years pass. Bonsai has become a true art form with a wide variety of styles, whose practise and popularity has spread worldwide.

A good bonsai composition must be beautiful, with harmony and balance between tree and container. True bonsai masterpieces may be hundreds of years old and are fascinating representations of natural trees in miniature form.

With such ancient traditions, it can be bewildering or even intimidating to know where to begin. Yet in today's world of ever-shrinking yards and green spaces, bonsai has probably never been so relevant. In fact, you need very little space or equipment to get started. All that is required is a little dedication, a good dose of patience, and some affinity and respect for plants.

This book is intended as an introduction to the hobby, and aims to help you to acquire the horticultural knowledge and artistic eye that bonsai demands. It will give guidance on how to buy and care for your bonsai, as well as information on some of the many species and styles that can be tried. Included in this kit are some of the essential items you will need to grow and create your own bonsai—training wire, cutters, and a bonsai dish. Hopefully, with this basic knowledge, you will be inspired to learn more about this ancient art and you will have discovered a rewarding hobby that will stay with you for years to come.

Opposite Top: The Japanese characters for Bonsai.
Opposite: A collected Juniper bonsai, sculpted mainly by the elements.
Right: This Juniper is over 100 years old.

HISTORY

CHINA

Gardening in China began as far back as the Shang Dynasty (18 BC to 12 BC). Bonsai was first developed in China and its origins are found in the Chinese love of the landscape, in particular their mountain scenery like that of the Guilen region in Southern China. The word "bonsai" comes from the Chinese words *pun sai* meaning "a landscape of rocks and trees in a tray" or more literally "tray scenery." The Chinese name for bonsai is *penjing* (potted landscape) and it is this landscape that is the main difference between Chinese and Japanese bonsai. In China the emphasis is on the landscape, whereas the Japanese have evolved the practice to concentrate on an individual tree.

In its beginning, *penjing* was very much the domain of the noble and wealthy. Chinese legend tells of an

emperor who created a miniature landscape of all the parts of his empire within his courtyard, so that he could stand and look out over all the lands that he ruled. It is also said that anyone else who was found to have a landscape in a dish was seen as a threat and put to death. The earliest evidence of bonsai is on wall paintings in the tomb of Prince Zhang Huai of the Tang Dynasty (AD 618–907). The paintings show servants carrying what appear to be a miniature landscape and a tree in a pot.

Mountains

In considering the importance of scenery in *penjing* it is vital to understand the significance of mountains to the Chinese. It could be said that *penjing* developed out of a love for mountains rather than trees. The Chinese mountain scenery is breathtaking, but their reverence for mountains has a religious aspect too. Many Chinese believe in the Immortals. There were supposedly eight Immortals who lived in the mountains. They visited the mortals occasionally but were rarely seen, giving them and their environment a mythical quality. The Taoists, who were among the original practitioners of bonsai, were obsessed with the Immortals and the mountains. Records dating as far back as the fifth century BC tell of Chinese scholars and poets visiting the mountains for inspiration. In the fourth century AD, a mandarin named Tong Kwo Ming abandoned his profession to grow

Opposite: A Chinese tomb painting of a servant carrying potted plants.

Left: Spectacular Chinese mountain scenery which inspired the art of bonsai.

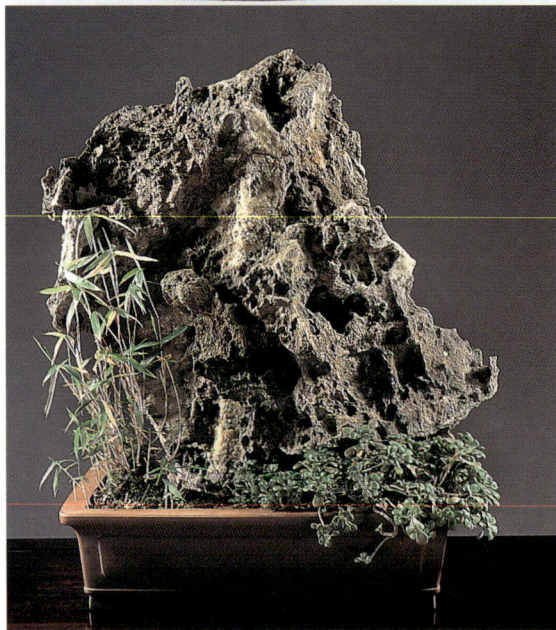

potted Chrysanthemums. Many other scholars also left the Imperial Court around this time, bound for the mountains to make gardens. This group is known as the "literati." They were a select group of artists and scholars who had a strong influence on Chinese art and bonsai, giving their name to one of the most expressive bonsai styles.

Stones

In the gardens created by the Chinese, miniature landscapes included rivers, lakes, mountains, and trees. Homage was paid to the mountains with the inclusion of found stones, resembling mountains and ranges.

Top: This multiple rock planting survives with nearly no soil.

Left: Chinese rock planting (*penjing*) with Dwarf Bamboo and Sedum.

From the making of these gardens, the study of such stones developed—Chinese "scholars' stones" or Japanese *suiseki*. Often displayed with bonsai, many of these stones had immense value. In Japan around AD 1650, a duke was said to have traded a castle for a particularly beautiful stone.

Religion

Religion also had a strong influence on *penjing*. The Taoists were obsessed with immortality and, in their search for an elusive elixir of life, they researched both plants and minerals. They believed that when an object was miniaturized, its energies were concentrated—so they dwarfed and thus prolonged the life of trees by slowing the rise of their sap.

Bonsai are found in Chinese and Japanese monasteries and it is the Zen Buddhist monks who are responsible for bringing bonsai to Japan. At one time *penjing* was thought to be too spiritually enriching for the masses, the reason given for its exclusivity to the nobility. As it did eventually permeate down through Chinese society and spread to the masses, bonsai also spread across physical boundaries. During the Kamakura period (AD 1185–1333) Zen Buddhism spread through Asia. The Zen Buddhist monks visited Japan from AD 794–1191 and their *penjing* came with them. Then, in the fourteenth century, the Chinese invaded Japan and brought with them many aspects of Chinese culture, including religion, calligraphy, and bonsai. Even today, the Chinese and Japanese symbols for bonsai remain the same.

JAPAN

In Japan, bonsai followed a similar path of development, starting in the monasteries before being taken up by the aristocracy. Originally trees were collected from the wild and people ventured high into the mountains to find the best specimens. Now few bonsai are collected this way as special permits are required, but their value as "natural" works of art is still considered to be far higher than plants grown from seed or cuttings.

Eventually, bonsai permeated through all levels of Japanese society as the nobility lost interest. As the working classes embraced the pastime, fashion dictated a change in emphasis toward flowers and colored leaves. Bonsai became part of Japanese life and for the first time they were displayed indoors.

By the seventeenth and eighteenth centuries, bonsai had become common in Japan. New styles were developed and new elements were included, such as additional plants, rocks, and small figurines. These mixed scenes are referred to as *bonkei,* while the production of realistic miniature landscapes similar to *penjing* is known as *saikei.*

Above: An example of penjing: fishermen under high cliffs. Note the tiny figures in the foreground: they are only ¼ in. high.

The journey west

Until the middle of the nineteenth century, bonsai was still only practiced in the East. Exhibitions held in Paris, Vienna, and London around the turn of the century exposed bonsai to the Western world for the first time.

The initial reaction was of shock and fascination. Bonsai was first perceived as cruel, with the dwarfed trees being tortured into shape. With the interest from the West came a new surge in popularity and soon there was a shortfall of wild material. Commercial bonsai production began and artists had to learn how to train cultivated plants to look like natural bonsai. With this came yet more adaptation of styles and the mastering of shaping techniques used commonly today.

Probably the last major influence in the globalization of bonsai was the Second World War. Returning American soldiers brought bonsai with them and the hobby spread across the U.S. and throughout the Western world.

Bonsai as art

Bonsai is an art form, not just a hobby. Its masterpieces have a visual impact on the viewer—they are wonderful compositions that truly look like the full-size trees they represent. Some are hundreds of years old and these have great historical, cultural, and monetary value. Currently the most expensive bonsai for sale is a Juniper "Rising Dragon" valued at $2,000,000. But unlike paintings or sculptures, bonsai are not finished works of art—they are living sculptures which continue to evolve. The care of older specimens may be passed from one generation to another; the bonsai outliving their masters. They require constant attention to maintain their beauty and are never complete. This dynamic quality, plus the fascination with the miniaturization process makes bonsai magical and their appeal enduring.

Below: This Larch was collected from the wild and planted on a rock. Note the detail of its cones.

Getting Started

EQUIPMENT *As with any hobby, there are a few things that you will need to get started.*

BASIC KIT

- Bonsai shears or secateurs for shaping and trimming foliage
- Angle cutters for removing branches
- Wire for shaping branches
- Wire cutters

Along with your basic kit (see left), you may also want a brush for cleaning the surface of the pot. Several different sizes of shears would also be useful. There are many different bonsai tools available, and the more involved you become, the more tools you will need. If you purchase a mature bonsai or one with a good shape, most of your work will be in maintenance—feeding, watering, and keeping the tree free of pests and diseases. If you make your own bonsai or reshape an existing plant, you may need to add more tools to your collection, such as branch benders, jinning pliers, and even power tools for carving and shaping.

POTS

Choose a pot that complements your tree but does not overpower it. Mature bonsai will remain in the same pot for years, but young plants will need repotting every two or three years. Flat, rectangular pots are most frequently used. They are available at specialist nurseries and often come from China, India, Japan, or Korea.

One to avoid—the graft on this small Pine is too high and the trunk is broader in the middle than at the base.

This Pyracantha is a garden center plant that would make good starter material for bonsai.

BUYING *Before you start to look, consider what you want to buy.*

Before buying your first bonsai, ask yourself the following questions. Is the bonsai going to be kept outdoors or indoors? How much space is available? Do you want a young tree or would you prefer to start off with a more mature specimen? How much do you want to spend? As a general rule, the older the bonsai, the more expensive it is likely to be. It may not be advisable to start with a really expensive specimen as your first bonsai—it would be devastating if it were lost due to inexperience or lack of time.

WHERE TO BUY

Avoid buying from department stores or indoor garden center shops where plants may have been sitting on a shelf or display stand for weeks in a hot, dry environment. Also avoid any packaged material: a plant in a cardboard box is difficult to water and will be lacking in light. It may be suffering or might not have survived at all.

If you are looking for ready-made bonsai material, whether mature specimens or work in progress, then you should seek out a specialist bonsai nursery. Here you will have access to a wide range of bonsai material and can benefit from the experience of bonsai experts. Good bonsai nurseries should be listed in your local telephone directory, and many also have their own websites. In addtion to trees, they will also have a range of tools, pots, compost, and books on the subject to help you.

If you are looking for untrained plant material to shape into your own bonsai, then garden centers and ordinary plant nurseries are a good place to look. Most of the plants here will come in container making them easier to transfer into bonsai pots later. Obviously, with this type of plant stock you will have much more work to do but this can be very rewarding.

WHAT TO LOOK FOR

Look for a healthy plant with a good shape, staying away from anything that looks weak or sickly. If you are buying a deciduous plant, it is safer not to buy during the winter months when the lack of leaves may disguise a bad choice. If the plant has been grafted, look for a good, clean, even joint that is not too high or too bulbous.

If you are buying from a garden center, look for plants with bushy growth and plenty of branches starting low down. Also look for plants with interestingly shaped trunks. These are often rejected by people looking for garden shrubs or trees and may end up in a bargain basement. However, as long as the plant is healthy, a crooked trunk adds to its potential as bonsai material, so this can be a good place to start.

This small Scots Pine does not look much in its black plastic pot.

The same tree is transformed once it has been planted in a bonsai dish.

BONSAI CARE

Like all container plants, bonsai need a certain amount of care to survive. Although a plant can live in a pot for many years, it needs feeding, trimming, and watering (in summer, water twice a day) on a regular basis to thrive. Your bonsai will also need shaping and repotting, and it is also vital to keep an eye out for pests.

YOUR FIRST BONSAI

Many people buy their first bonsai as a kit in a box. Unfortunately, these do not always fare very well. Too often the new bonsai owner places the plant on a windowsill and watches it die. This may be because a plant that has been sitting in a box is not necessarily going to be healthy—it will be lacking light and water. Location is also an important consideration. Many bonsai are sold as houseplants, but this is a misconception. Most species are actually outdoor plants and as such should live outside. Whether it is an indoor or outdoor bonsai, you need to provide the following:

- A stable environment without too much variation in light or heat
- Regular watering and feeding
- Good air circulation
- A close watch for pests and diseases

INDOOR BONSAI

The only true indoor bonsai are plants that come from tropical or semi-tropical climates and will not survive cold temperatures. Place the bonsai in a stable environment without extremes of heat or light. Cool but humid rooms are good, so try a spare room or bathroom. Because the supply of light is limited indoors, turn your bonsai regularly to avoid it leaning toward the light. If you have a large bonsai, consider buying a turntable to make turning easier. Your bonsai will be happy on a shelf or windowsill, but make sure the temperature does not fluctuate too much. Don't close the drapes in front of the tree at night or the cold pocket of air around the bonsai can lead to leaf drop or death. If the climate allows, the bonsai can live outside in the summer, but watch for pests and diseases and bring it back inside before the weather turns cold.

OUTDOOR BONSAI

Outside, bonsai will need the same level of care as any potted plants. Avoid excessive winds or direct midday sun which can scorch or defoliate trees. In winter, strong, dehydrating winds can kill a bonsai. You may need to create a simple windbreak and shade structure from timber and shade netting. As with indoor trees, turn your bonsai regularly to avoid any lean toward the light. Try not to place your bonsai against a fence or wall, as this prevents good air circulation which can lead to disease. If you live in a wet climate, tilt your bonsai to avoid waterlogging by putting a wedge under one side of the pot. Keep moving the wedge to different sides of the pot to ensure the water drains evenly and does not collect in one corner.

HOW TO TURN A GARDEN CENTER PLANT INTO BONSAI

1. Having found a suitable plant to make into a bonsai, repot it into a shallow, bonsai-style container. Remove about a third of the existing rootball.

2. Reduce the top growth of the plant by a similar amount so that there is not too much plant for the reduced root system to support. As you do this, think about the shape of the bonsai.

3. Wire the branches to improve the shape of the plant if necessary.

4. Until it is established, treat the plant with extra care, giving it protection against the elements, perhaps in a cool greenhouse.

Below, from far left:
This 36 in. pine was bought in a garden center and repotted into a seed tray. It was then pruned and its branches wired. When it was repotted into a bonsai pot, it really started to take shape. The training will continue for years. The picture directly below shows a garden center plant after four years.

READY-MADE BONSAI
When buying a ready-made bonsai, choose a specimen that looks like a miniature tree for the best start.

Looking closely at the plant, you should focus on the following areas:

Trunk This should ideally taper from the base of the plant to the crown. Check for scars left by bad pruning—although branches will have been removed in the shaping of the tree, this should not leave ugly scars. Many bonsai are formed by reducing the height of a larger tree, by cutting out its top. If this is done well, the cut should be angled and will, in time, blend into the trunk and become less obvious. A bad cut will be horizontal and square in appearance—this type of scar will always stand out.

A collection of Literati Scots Pines.

QUESTIONS TO ASK:

• When was the tree potted or repotted? If the soil is mounded up above the rim of the pot, it was repotted recently. It is important to know, as a growing bonsai will need repotting every two to three years.

• Where has the plant come from? If it has been transported a distance, has it had time to acclimatize? Some plants arrive rootballed in clay or with their roots washed. Once they are potted, they need time to adjust.

• Does the plant require any special care? Get as much information about the history and care of the plant as possible. This is particularly important with large and expensive specimens.

A group planting of Larches on a piece of slate.

A 15-year-old Weeping Willow.

Roots The roots of your bonsai should be visible on the surface of the pot. The overall appearance should be natural and, as with the branches, there should be no ugly scars made by pruning. The plant should be stable in its pot—a good test for this is to see if you can rock it in its pot. If you can, then it has probably been recently potted or repotted and should be avoided. A reputable bonsai nursery should be happy to demonstrate that their stock is well-potted by lifting them out of their containers. The plant should lift easily and once the rootball is visible it should be easy to see the white tips of the roots at its edges.

Branches The overall branch structure of the tree is perhaps more important than the shape of the crown. The foliage can be trimmed and shaped, but a weak branch structure is impossible to change. Look for well-spaced, natural-looking branches and avoid any plant that appears either leggy or too congested.

Wiring If you are looking at bonsai that are in training, they will probably be wired. Do not buy a plant if the wire is cutting into the bark, as this will permanently scar the branches.

Compost Check that the compost in the pot is not too dry or waterlogged—it should be moist to the touch but not soggy. Moss on the surface of the compost is acceptable, but do not buy a plant that has lots of weeds, as this illustrates a lack of care.

POPULAR STYLES *There are many different styles of bonsai and some are more complex and difficult to achieve than others. It is worth finding out more about specific styles and their rules, so that you can perfect the branch structure, placement, and overall shape.*

above
A juniper in Semi-Cascade style.
opposite
This Driftwood-style Chinese Juniper is over 100 years old.

Formal Upright style Bonsai of this style should have a completely straight stem and be conical in shape. This sounds simple, but it is a very rigid form with precise rules on the positioning of the branches that make it one of the most difficult styles to achieve. These bonsai emulate trees growing in the middle of fields. With no competition for light, water, or food, they grow up straight and tall.

Informal Upright style Similar to the Formal Upright Style in overall shape, the easiest way to describe this style is having a trunk shaped like a lazy "S." This is probably the most popular and easiest style to start off with as it is easy to find trees or shrubs with a natural bend to their stems.

Root Over Rock style With this style, most of the focus is, as the name suggests, on the look of the roots. It can be difficult to achieve and it may take up to ten years to

above, from left:
A Hornbeam trained in the Semi-Cascade style, a group planting of Sawara Cypresses, and a Trident Maple grown in the Root Over Rock style.

establish a good bonsai of this style. The roots of the tree are draped over the rock and tied on with string or wire; it can take a long time for them to take hold.

Planted On Rock style In this style, the rocks represent mountains and should be vertical to the container. The tree is planted into the rock in a crevice so that it looks like it has seeded there. The plant should not overpower or obscure the beauty of the rock. These bonsai are displayed in a flat dish containing either water or sand.

WIRING

Most bonsai are wired to alter or improve their shape.

You will need a range of different gauges of wire for different parts of the tree. There are two main types:
Copper This needs to be annealed (made soft). You can buy annealed wire, but this can also be easily done by burning it in a small fire. Copper wire hardens when bent and when exposed to the elements, so a relatively small gauge may be used to hold branches.
Aluminum This is less expensive than copper. It is slightly more difficult to bend, but equally strong. and it is sometimes possible to reuse it.

WHEN TO WIRE

It is easiest to wire during winter and early spring when plants are dormant. Check the tree frequently to ensure the wire is not biting into the bark. If the plant is growing vigorously, replace the wire frequently. As ageneral rule, leave wires in place for three months.

REMOVING THE WIRE

Always use cutters to remove wire. Do not be tempted to unwind the wire off the tree as it is very easy to damage or knock off leaf and flower buds this way.

PROTECTION

On very young or very old specimens, protect the branch from contact with the wire. Soak some raffia in water, then apply to the branch or trunk prior to wiring.

A Trident Maple being reshaped. Note the wiring on the branches.

HOW TO WIRE

1. The wire should be about 50% longer than the branch or trunk to be wired.

2. Secure the wire to another branch or push it into the soil between the roots if you are wiring the trunk.

3. Start from the thickest part of the branch or trunk and work outward toward the thinnest part.

4. Wiring should be evenly spaced at an angle of around 45° to the branch.

5. The wire should barely touch the surface of the bark. If it is too loose, it will have no effect—if it is too tight, it will cut into the branch.

6. Wiring may be clockwise or counterclockwise, but take care not to cross two wires running in different directions as this can block the movement of sap through the branch or trunk.

7. If you are wiring two branches that are opposite each other, try to use one piece of wire.

8. If one wire is not strong enough, then a second can be placed next to it.

9. If you are rewiring a branch or trunk, make sure that the wire sits in a slightly different position to the original wire. This way there is less chance of marking the bark as the pressure from the wire is not exerted on the same spot.

10. Leave extra wire at the end of the branch to allow for growth.

11. Bend the trunk or branch into shape using your thumbs. Do not exert too much pressure—you don't want to cause a break.

DOS AND DON'TS

DOS

1. Wiring should coil around the branch at 45° and be evenly spaced.

2. If you need to apply a second wire to a branch, it should be placed directly next to the first wire.

3. If you are wiring two branches opposite each other, a single piece of wire may be used.

DON'TS

4. Wires should not cross in opposite directions—this can damage or strangle the branch.

5. Be careful not to wire your branches too tightly.

6. If wiring is too far apart, it will have no effect.

7. If wiring is too loose, it will have no effect.

PRUNING

Bonsai need to be both trimmed and pruned to achieve and maintain their shapes. As in normal gardening, beginners are sometimes afraid to prune.

If left unpruned, plants—bonsai or otherwise—lose their shape and vigor. So pruning is not cruel but in fact beneficial to the plant.

To remove small- to medium-sized branches, use secateurs or cutters. When removing large branches, use a pruning saw and make a shallow cut from underneath before sawing off the branch from the top. This way there is less risk of tearing the bark.

• Keep cutting tools sharp and clean.
• Make cuts at right angles to the trunk or branch to be kept.
• Approach the branch from the side, not from above or below.

WHEN TO PRUNE

The best time to prune is when the tree is dormant, that is when the sap is not rising. This generally means from late fall to early spring. The timing varies from species to species but as a general rule:

• Prune deciduous trees in late winter to early spring before the buds start to break.

• Prune evergreens and conifers in winter to early spring.

• Prune Pines in the late fall.

• Prune Japanese Maples in mid winter.

TRIMMING

Through the season, as trees put on new growth, they need trimming to keep their shape. As this will be relatively soft growth, secateurs or even sharp scissors may be used. There are no hard-and-fast rules for trimming, but as a quick guide, to maintain shape you will need to think of the foliage of the tree in thirds.

The top third of the tree should be trimmed quite hard, back to the first set of leaves on the leaf stalk. The middle section of the tree should be trimmed to the second set of leaves, while the bottom section should be lightly pruned, to the third set of leaves. This method allows growth to taper toward the apex of the tree. In practice, you may actually just lightly prune the entire tree—it is simply a case of standing back and looking at the composition and using your judgment.

DEFOLIATING

To achieve smaller leaves and strong fall color, a tree may be defoliated (stripped of its leaves) early in the season. This forces the plant to produce a second set of leaves in the same season. The leaves are cut off at the stalk in early to mid summer. This is only really suitable for deciduous trees and should never be done later than this. It should also not be done on a tree in two consecutive years or tried on a tree that is not growing strongly. This method can be used to try to save a plant that has been scorched by strong sun.

REPOTTING *Because bonsai are kept in relatively small containers as part of the dwarfing process of the trees, they soon become pot bound and need to be repotted.*

Repot when the roots fill the pot and have no more room to expand. This will be every two to three years, or four years for mature specimens. As long as the tree and pot are still in proportion, reuse the existing pot. If the tree has grown or been radically reshaped, you may need to find a new pot.

1. Remove the bonsai from its pot. It should lift out without too much effort.

2. Loosen and untangle the roots using a fork or hook. When the tree is repotted, it should also have its roots pruned and compost replaced. This allows the tree to take up valuable nutrients, air, and water.

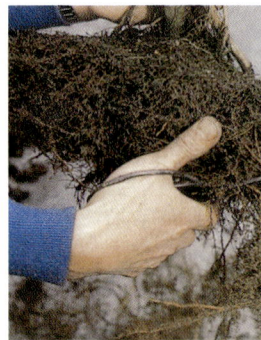

3. Reduce the size of the rootball by cutting off excess roots with a pair of sharp scissors or secateurs. You should remove enough so that the rootball will fit in its container with 1in of space around the edges.

4. Cover the drainage holes in the bottom of the pot with plastic mesh so that they do not become clogged with compost.

5. Put a layer of compost, about 1/2 in. deep, in the bottom of the pot.

6. Place the tree on top of the compost. Make sure it is at the right height in the pot and at the right angle and position.

7. Fill around the plant with compost. Press it down firmly to make sure there are no air pockets.

8. Mound the compost up above the rim as it will sink later. Water immediately, and again as it dries out. Give the tree extra protection for two weeks.

COMPOST

There are branded bonsai composts which are available from specialist nurseries:

- **Akadama** is suitable for general use.
- **Kureyu** is used for conifers.
- **Kanuma** is used for Azaleas, Maples, and other acid-loving plants.

If you prefer to mix up your own bonsai compost, make sure it is soil-based and free-draining. Try a mixture of soil, sand or grit, and organic matter such as leaf mold or well-rotted garden compost.

Pests and Diseases

The first rule of pest and disease care is that prevention is better than cure. It is far better to avoid a problem altogether if possible. It is therefore vital to get into good habits for hygiene and general plant care—in doing so, you can avoid many potential problems. However, if you do encounter a problem, do not panic as most can be easily dealt with either organically or with the use of chemicals. If you follow this quick guide to pest and disease prevention, however, any problem you encounter shouldn't be too serious.

PREVENTION

- **Watering** Keep plants well watered; don't let them dry out. If the roots dry out, the tree can't take up nutrients or water from the soil and is put under stress. Do not allow the plant to sit in water as this can cause the roots to rot and harbor disease. Tilt the pot to allow extra drainage, if necessary.

- **Air** Space your plants so they don't touch either each other or any nearby walls or fences. Allow air circulation around the plants.

- **Repotting** Repot regularly and don't let your plants become pot-bound. If the roots have entirely filled the pot, the plant cannot take up nutrients or water from the compost.

Top: Powdered fertilizer is applied to the soil.
Above: Bonsai planted on rocks should be fed with a liquid fertilizer.

- **Feeding** Feed your bonsai regularly through the growing period (early spring to late summer). The best time to feed is in the early morning or evening when there is no strong sunlight. Water your bonsai before you apply food, and only use the recommended dosage. Don't be tempted to overdose a plant if it is not growing strongly—too much fertilizer can damage the plant by burning the roots. If you are using specialist bonsai fertilizer, follow the instructions on the package. If you are using ordinary garden or houseplant food, it is better to use it at half the suggested strength and feed twice as often. If you prefer to use pelleted food, then apply it when repotting or place on the compost surface where it will be released gradually when the plant is watered. Be sure not to feed or excessively water a repotted bonsai for at least three weeks after it has been repotted.

- **Pruning** Ensure all pruning tools are kept clean and consider washing in a fungicide solution between uses. Clean tools will minimize the spread of disease between plants.

- **Hygiene** Keep the compost surface and the area around the bonsai clean. Remove dropped leaves as soon as possible—diseased leaves spread problems to other plants and decomposing leaves can harbor harmful insects. Remove weeds from the surface of the compost as they create competition for the limited supply of water, light, and nutrients available to the container plant.

Above: Verticillium wilt.

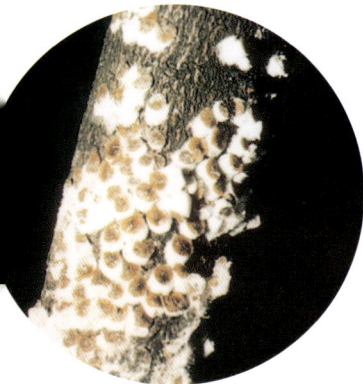

Above: Scale insects clustered on a branch.

PROBLEMS

Despite good care and hygiene, problems do still occur. Some of the most common problems are:

Rust

Affects: Oak, Birch, Alder, Scots Pine, European Five-needled Pine, Larch, Juniper.
Symptoms: Yellow or orange spots and blisters appear on the leaves.

Rust is actually very difficult to control once it has set in, although chemicals can be used to stop it spreading. It is important to remove all affected leaves and dispose of them by burning to prevent spread.

Verticillium Wilt

Affects: Predominantly Acers.
Symptoms: Trees wilt or die suddenly with no apparent reason. Cut into a stem and you will see dark brown bands running through it.

This disease is only really diagnosable after the plant has died, so there is little that can be done to prevent it. This sometimes occurs where a plant has been in an outside planting bed. In this case, you should dig up the bed in which it was planted and then fumigate the soil.

Needle Cast

Affects: Scots, European, and Oriental Pines, and occasionally Larches.
Symptoms: Small brown spots appear alongside thin black lines, mainly on the young needles. These diseased young needles are then shed in the fall when normally just the older needles drop. A bad case of needle cast can defoliate an entire tree. Treat it with a fungicide.

Gray Mold

Affects: Maples, Larches, Cypresses, Cryptomeria.
Symptoms: Gray mold on the new growth.

This is due to bad hygiene, dead leaves lying around, and overcrowded growing conditions. It can be treated with fungicide, and if the hygiene problems are dealt with too, the problem should go away.

Mildew

Affects: mainly deciduous species, especially Acers.
Symptoms: similar to gray mold, although mildew is more of a white color. Hairy gray to white powdery deposits are found on the plant. There may be tiny white spots with powdery mildew.

Again, this is caused by poor hygiene or growing conditions, in particular poor air circulation and excess wetness and humidity. Treat with a fungicide and try to improve the growing conditions.

Galls

Affects: most deciduous trees, particularly Oaks (Spangle Gall).
Symptoms: Galls (small domes or disks) appear on the surface of leaves.

Chemicals are secreted on the plant by midge and wasp larvae. These larvae make the plant form the galls that enclose the larvae and protect them until they hatch. The galls can be picked off if they are unsightly, or left as they cause no real harm to the plant.

Insects

Insects will attack many different types of plants. The best prevention is to be vigilant. There are three types of insects: Borers which feed on the roots

Above: Bonsai are a popular subject for painting.

Right: Galls.

Above: Winter moth larvae.

and stems of plants, leaf cutters which feed on the leaves, roots, and stems of plants, and lastly leaf and stem suckers which feed by sucking on the leaves and stems.

Borers are the larvae of moths, weevils, and beetles. They burrow into the roots and stems of plants. Perhaps the best known is the vine weevil larvae which can do devastating damage. It is often found in the roots of container plants and you should keep an eye out for the grubs when repotting.

Leaf cutters are perhaps easiest to spot as the damage that they do is the most visible, such as notches taken out of leaves. They can often just be picked off a plant.

Leaf and stem suckers: The two most common are probably aphids and scale insects. Aphids can be sprayed or sometimes washed off plants. Scale insects, which are small brown or white pod-like insects found on twigs and branches, can be either picked off (although this is not the most pleasant job) or sprayed to remove them.

Visible insects on bonsai can be dealt with by insecticides, biological control, or simply by removing and either squashing them or moving them to another part of the garden.

You can also spray insecticides at regular intervals through the growing season to catch both the eggs and young that are not visible to the naked eye before they infest a plant.

Above: Common Spangle Gall.

TREATMENTS

Chemicals

If you use fungicides and insecticides to combat pests and diseases, either by watering or spraying, as a guide these should be applied once a month, but not at the same time. The laws governing chemicals are different in each country. Refer to a specialist bonsai nursery or a good garden center for advice on what to use, how, and when. When handling chemicals, take care to read all the instructions carefully, and use them in a well-ventilated area, maybe wearing a mask to avoid breathing in spray. Always wash your hands after use. Systemics are preferable as they are absorbed and carried to all parts of the plant.

Organics

If you prefer to avoid the use of chemicals, then you need to place an even greater emphasis on plant care and hygiene to avoid problems. There is a lot of information available on organic gardening both in books and on the internet. It is worthwhile looking into companion plantings to draw away insect pests. For the removal of pests, perhaps the best organic option is biological control, where parasites are used to combat problem insects.

Left: A healthy Juniper with beautiful driftwood.

Species Guide

The following section is a brief reference guide to some of the trees available and suitable for making into bonsai. For ease of use, the species have been separated into deciduous species, listed first, and evergreen species. Information is included for each species which covers applicable bonsai styles, hardiness, growing conditions, and preferred compost type. There is also a brief guide to feeding and watering requirements, and some of the common pest and disease problems that may occur.

BARBERRY (*Berberis*)

These are small-leaved, spiny, deciduous or evergreen shrubs. Their natural habitat is rocky mountainsides around the Northern hemisphere, Northern and tropical areas of Africa, and South America. They produce red or orange flowers in spring, followed by shiny red fruits in the fall. Deciduous varieties also have good fall leaf color.

Species and varieties used: Predominantly Berberis thunbergii *and its cultivars. Evergreen species do not work well.*

Bonsai styles: *Informal Upright styles and group plantings.*

Hardiness: *These are very hardy shrubs that withstand temperatures of 14°F to 90°F.*

Position: *Full sun or partial shade.*

Compost: *General-purpose compost is adequate, with a 60/40 mix of organic matter to grit.*

Feed: *Use a general-purpose fertilizer through spring and summer, and a low-nitrogen feed in fall.*

Water: *Keep the compost moist throughout the growing season.*

Pests and diseases: *No major problems, but Barberries may be attacked by aphids or suffer from mildew if growing conditions are not ideal.*

Berberis thunbergii.

BEECH (*Fagus*)

These are large deciduous forest trees from the Northern hemisphere, whose leaves turn a wonderful coppery brown in the fall and are held on the tree over winter.

Species and varieties used: *Most popular are* Fagus sylvatica *(Common or European Beech) and its purple-leaved version* Fagus sylvatica 'Purpurea' *(Purple or Copper Beech).* Fagus crenata *(White or Japanese Beech) is also useful for bonsai as it has smaller leaves.*

Bonsai styles: *Formal and Informal Upright styles.*

Hardiness: *These plants are very hardy (14°F to 80°F) but are not suitable for constantly hot climates. If the temperature is regularly over 85°F, the tree will suffer. Beeches need protection over prolonged periods of freezing weather of 14°F and below.*

Position: *Full sun or partial shade.*

Common Beech (*Fagus sylvatica*) in winter.

Compost: *General-purpose compost with a 60/40 mixture of organic matter to grit is best.*

Feed: *Apply a balanced fertilizer in spring and summer but don't feed them straight away in spring—wait until about a month after the leaves emerge. Use a nitrogen-free feed from late summer through to fall, stopping when the leaves begin to change color.*

Water: *Keep the compost moist all year round and water frequently in spring and summer. Don't allow the compost to dry out or the plant will suffer.*

Pests and diseases: *Can be attacked by aphids, scale insects, and mildew.*

BIRD PLUM
(*Sageretia theezans*)

These are tender evergreen shrubs (deciduous in temperate climates) popular in subtropical areas. The branches and trunk flake, leaving attractive pale patches on the gray trunk. This plant has small leaves and an angular growth pattern with sharp bends in the branches.

Species and varieties used: Sageretia theezans.
Bonsai styles: *Informal styles, also Semi and Full Cascade.*
Hardiness: *Tender (54°F to 98°F). Needs at least 64°F to grow well.*
Position: *Partial shade, indoors or outdoors.*
Compost: *General-purpose compost with a 60/40 mixture of organic matter to grit is best.*
Feed: *Apply a balanced fertilizer from spring until fall. Stop feeding when the growth stops in fall and recommence a couple of weeks after the tree starts growing again in spring.*
Water: *Needs plenty of water in the growing season from spring to fall. Keep the compost moist throughout winter. Spray the foliage once a day.*

Pests and diseases: *Prone to suffer from aphids, red spider mites, and mineral deficiencies.*

Bird Plum trained in the Split Trunk style.

COTONEASTER

This genus includes mainly deciduous trees and shrubs which can be used as creepers or ground cover, wall shrubs, or garden shrubs. They have white or pink flowers in spring, followed by handsome red fruit in the fall.

Species and varieties used: *Mainly* Cotoneaster horizontalis, *but also* Cotoneaster dammeri, Cotoneaster franchettii, Cotoneaster microphyllus, *and* Cotoneaster simonsii.

Bonsai styles: *Very useful for Mame bonsai and most Informal styles including Horizontal, Cascades, and groupings with rocks.*

Hardiness: *Hardy from 27°F to 90°F, but does not like very cold winds.*
Position: *Full sun.*
Compost: *Use a general-purpose compost, with a 50/50 mix of organic matter to grit.*
Feed: *Apply a balanced feed in spring and summer, and a nitrogen-free feed in late summer and fall.*

Water: *Cotoneasters do not like too much water, so you should allow the compost almost to dry out between waterings in summer, and keep the compost just moist through winter.*
Pests and diseases: *These plants are particularly prone to attack by aphids and red spider mites.*

This 25- to 30-year-old Cotoneaster is only 10 in. tall

A group planting of Cotoneaster.

A Crab Apple trained in the Informal Upright style.

14°F to 77°F. If the temperature regularly exceeds 86°F, the tree will be stressed but it should survive. They need protection in prolonged spells of freezing weather.
Position: Full sun.
Compost: Use a general-purpose compost or clay-based loam with a 70/30 mix of organic matter to grit. It is also worth using slightly deeper pots than with other species to conserve moisture.
Feed: Apply a balanced feed in spring and summer, and a nitrogen-free feed in fall.
Water: Water well in summer when the plant is forming fruits, keep very moist in spring and fall, and maintain even levels of moisture through winter.
Pests and diseases: Crab Apples are prone to attack from aphids, mildew, and apple canker.

CRAB APPLE (*Malus*)

Small ornamental trees grown for their blossom and colorful fall fruits (which are mostly inedible). These are among the main flowering plants used for bonsai.

Species and varieties used: *Mainly* Malus cerasifera *and* Malus halliana *(Hall's Crab Apple), but you may also come across:* Malus baccata *(Siberian Crab Apple),* Malus floribunda *(Japanese Crab Apple),* Malus hupehensis, Malus micromalus *(which has very small fruit),* Malus sargentii, *and* Malus sieboldii.

Bonsai styles: *Informal and Formal Upright styles as well as some other Informal styles.*

Hardiness: *Hardy from*

ELM (*Ulmus*)

These are tall, narrow, upright trees which were used prolifically in avenues and hedging until the outbreak of Dutch Elm Disease. They flower before they come into leaf and as a result look like they are about to break into leaf very early. Suckers are formed easily at the base of the tree.

Species and varieties used: Most forms can be made into bonsai, but the most commonly seen are Ulmus parviflora *(Chinese Elm,* which has several forms with cork-like bark), Ulmus plotii *(Plot Elm, named after Dr. Plot),* and Ulmus procera *(English or Field Elm).* Ulmus x elegantissima *'Jacqueline Hillier' is a good bonsai tree as it has small leaves and compact growth.*

Bonsai styles: *Informal Upright styles and group plantings.*

Hardiness: *Hardy from 27°F to 90°F but the Chinese Elm is less hardy than the European. At winter temperatures of 45–50°F, Elms will not drop their leaves.*

A Plot Elm being trained as a Formal Upright bonsai.

Position: *Full sun to partial shade. Can be grown indoors in partial shade.*

Compost: *General-purpose compost with a 60/40 mix of organic matter to grit.*

Feed: *Apply a balanced feed from spring until late summer, and a nitrogen-free feed in late summer until leaf drop in fall. If kept indoors, use a balanced fertilizer at half strength through winter.*

Water: *Water well through spring and summer and maintain an even level of moisture through fall and winter, less if the leaves have dropped.*

Pests and diseases: *Elms may suffer from aphids, scale insects, red spider mites, and mildew. It is not advisable to use systemic insecticides or fungicides on Elms.*

HORNBEAM (*Carpinus*)

These large, deciduous trees are similar in appearance to Beech, but their leaves are narrower with strong veins. Although they turn a similar coppery brown color in the fall, the leaves do not remain on the tree through winter.

Species and varieties used:
Carpinus laxiflora
(Japanese Hornbeam),
Carpinus turczaninovii
*(Korean Hornbeam which
has good fall color), and*
Carpinus betulus *(Common
Hornbeam).*

Bonsai styles: *Formal and
Informal Upright styles.
Sometimes also planted
as groups.*

Hardiness: *Hardy from
around 23°F or below to
90°F. It will withstand
freezing temperatures but
give it protection in cold
spells of over a week and
avoid drying winds.*

Position: *Full sun to partial
shade. If the bonsai is in
full sun, shade the pot.*

Compost: *General-purpose
compost with a 60/40 mix
of organic matter to grit.*

Feed: *Use a balanced feed
from spring until the middle*

Hornbeam
(*Carpinus betulus*).

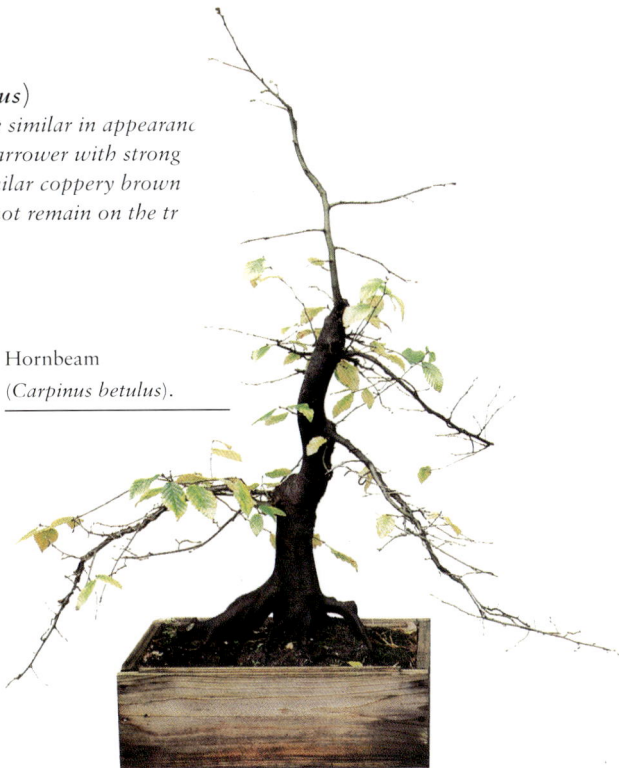

of summer. Then switch to
a nitrogen-free feed until
the tree drops its leaves.

Water: *Water Hornbeams
well through the growing
season and do not allow the
compost to dry even a little.
Reduce amounts of water
in fall and keep just moist
through the winter.*

Pests and diseases: *Prone
to attack by aphids and
mildew. Small toadstools
may appear at the base of
the tree but these are not a
problem as they are the
fruiting bodies of a fungus
that lives side by side with
the tree and helps it to
absorb nutrients.*

LARCH (*Larix*)

These deciduous conifers grow naturally as forest trees in the Northern hemisphere. In cultivation they are used as both specimen trees and topiary, grafted onto clear stems of another species. They have good fall color as their leaves fade to yellow before dropping, and fresh green growth in spring. Trees over 10 years old should produce cones that will remain in the tree for several years.

Species and varieties used: Larix leptolepis *(Japanese Larch)* has a reddish fall and winter color. Larix decidua *(European Larch)* has a yellow fall and winter color. Larix x eurolepis *(Dunkeld Larch)* has attractive cones. **Bonsai styles:** *Many different Informal styles, Upright styles, and group plantings are used.*

A group planting of seven European Larch.

Hardiness: *Hardy from around 23°F to 90°F.*
Position: *Partial shade. Protect the leaves from burning in strong sun.*
Compost: *Use a 60/40 mix of organic matter to grit, or alternatively equal amounts of Akadama and Kureyu composts.*
Feed: *Start with a nitrogen-rich feed in spring and stop feeding altogether in the middle of summer. In late summer switch to a low-nitrogen feed until fall.*
Water: *Keep the compost moist through the year.*
Pests and diseases: *Prone to aphids and mildew.*

Fall color displayed on a Japanese Larch.

This example
of *Ginkgo biloba* from china
is over 150 years old.

MAIDENHAIR TREE (*Ginkgo biloba*)

This deciduous conifer is one of the oldest species of plant known. It is a narrow, upright tree which spreads as it ages. Its distinctive leaves are similar to the Maidenhair Fern and turn a golden yellow in fall.

Ginkgo does not respond well to pruning and will often die back, which makes it a challenging bonsai plant.

Species and varieties used: Ginkgo biloba. *In Japan, fruit-bearing varieties such as 'Chichi Icho' are used.*

Bonsai styles: *It is not used in a wide range of styles*

due to its particular growth habit. Ginkgo is best shaped into Upright styles and group plantings.

Hardiness: *Hardy from around 23°F to 90°F. It will withstand frost but prefers some protection over winter.*

Position: *Full sun to partial shade.*

Compost: *Use a general-purpose compost with a 70/30 mix of organic matter to grit.*

Feed: *Use a balanced feed from late spring until summer, and a nitrogen-free feed from early fall until the leaves have dropped.*

Water: *Water well in spring and summer and spray the foliage frequently. Reduce watering in fall and just keep the compost moist in winter.*

Pests and diseases: *Prone to attacks from aphids, scale insects, and mildew.*

MAPLES (*Acer*)

Maples are probably the best-known and most widely used deciduous trees and shrubs for bonsai. They are renowned for their stunning fall leaf colors and some species and varieties have equally colorful leaves in spring. The leaf shapes and colors, and fascinating barks, of this family of trees are diverse and they sometimes produce winged fruits after their insignificant flowers.

Species and varieties used:
*The main species are the Trident Maples (*Acer buergerianum*) and the Japanese Maples (*Acer palmatum *and *Acer japonicum*). Other popular plants are *Acer campestre *(Field Maple), *Acer capillipes *(Snake Bark Maple), *Acer circinatum *(Vine Leaf Maple), *Acer ginnala *(Amur Maple), Acer griseum *(Paper Bark Maple), *Acer platanoides *(Norway Maple), *Acer pseudoplatanus *(Sycamore), and *Acer rubrum *(Red Maple).*
Bonsai styles: *Acers are generally seen as Informal Upright styles. Trident Maples work well in Root over Rock style and also in group plantings.*

Trident Maple

Acer buergerianum *has three-lobed maple leaves.*
Hardiness: *Hardy from around 32°F to 86°F. It is only really possible to grow this plant in temperate areas, not in the tropics or subtropics, as it does not like prolonged hot weather. It will take a certain amount of freezing for short periods but needs protection over long spells.*
Position: *Full sun or partial shade.*
Compost: *Use a general-purpose bonsai soil with a 60/40 mix of organic matter to grit.*
Feed: *Apply a balanced general-purpose feed in the growing season and replace with a nitrogen-free feed in late summer and fall.*

A group planting of Trident Maple (*Acer buergerianum*).

Water: *Water well in spring and summer, reduce in fall, keep just moist in winter.*
Pests and diseases: *May suffer from aphids, mildew, and powdery mildew.*

Japanese Maple

Acer japonicum *has leaves with 7 to 11 lobes, while *Acer palmatum *has leaves with 5 to 7 lobes.*

Species and varieties used:
Acer palmatum 'Deshojo' has leaves which open bright red and fade to green through the season.
Acer palmatum 'Kiyohime' is a green-leaved variety which spreads horizontally.
Acer palmatum 'Seigen' has leaves that open bright red, turn to a coral pink color, then become green edged with orange. In fall they are bright red.

Hardiness: Hardy from around 32°F to 86°F. It is only really possible to grow these maples in temperate areas, not in the tropics or subtropics, as they do not like prolonged hot weather—it will cause the plant to shut down. They will take freezing temperatures for short periods, but need protection over prolonged periods.

Opposite and above:
Japanese Maples (Acer palmatum) are prized for their branch structure, shown here in winter without leaves.

Position: Partial shade out of strong winds.
Compost: Slightly acidic compost is needed. Akadama compost is fine, with a 60/40 mix of organic matter to grit.
Feed: Feed Japanese Maples with a balanced general-purpose fertilizer through spring and summer, and change to a low-nitrogen feed in the fall.
Water: Keep the compost evenly moist all year round. Japanese Maples do not enjoy excesses of either dry or wet.
Pests and diseases: Can be prone to attacks from aphids, red spider mites, and powdery mildew.

Common Oak
(*Quercus robur*).

Species and varieties used:
Quercus robur *(English Oak) and* Quercus ilex *(Evergreen or Holm Oak).*
Bonsai styles: *Usually single specimens in Formal or Informal styles.*
Hardiness: *Hardy from around 14°F to 86°F. Protection is needed in prolonged periods of freezing weather.*
Position: *Full sun to partial shade. Keep the pot shaded if sited in full sun.*
Compost: *Use a general-purpose compost with a 60/40 mix of organic matter to grit. Alternatively, mix 50% Akadama, 30% soil-less compost, and 20% grit.*
Feed: *Use a balanced feed in the growing season.*
Water: *Water thoroughly in summer, keep moist through spring and fall, and slightly damp in winter.*
Pests and diseases: *Aphids, mildew, and galls can be a problem with Oaks.*

OAK (*Quercus*)

These are large deciduous woodland trees, some with excellent fall leaf color. Those species found mainly in the Northern hemisphere have smooth bark, whereas Oaks from warmer climates tend to have cork-like bark. Acorns are formed on most varieties in the fall.

SOUTHERN BEECH
(*Nothofagus*)

These large deciduous and evergreen trees originate in the Southern hemisphere, where they can be found growing wild in forests. They are similar in appearance to Beech and Hornbeam. The deciduous varieties are known for their good fall color.

Species and varieties used: Nothofagus antarctica *(Antarctic Beech or Nirre)*, Nothofagus procera *(Rauli).*
Bonsai styles: *Formal and Informal styles as specimens or in groups.*
Hardiness: *Southern Beech is hardy from 23°F to around 86°F.*
Position: *Full sun or partial shade.*
Compost: *General-purpose compost with a 60/40 mix of organic matter to grit.*
Feed: *Use a balanced feed in spring and summer. Switch to a nitrogen-free feed from later summer until the tree drops its leaves.*

Water: *Plenty of water in spring and summer. Keep moist all year round.*
Pests and diseases: *Aphids, scale insects, and mildew can cause problems.*

Antarctic Beech
(*Nothofagus antarctica*).

WILLOW (*Salix*)

Willows are deciduous trees and shrubs varying in size. They have flexible stems and most produce attractive catkins in late winter and early spring. They are also early to come into leaf and very quick growing. Some varieties have colorful winter stems.

Species and varieties used: *Most commonly used for bonsai are* Salix babylonica *(Weeping Willow),* Salix caprea *(Goat Willow),* Salix fragilis *(Crack Willow), and* Salix x sepulcralis 'Chrysocoma' *(Golden Weeping Willow).*

Bonsai styles: *Upright Informal styles and Weeping styles.*

Hardiness: *Willows are fully hardy from around 14°F to around 86°F.*

Position: *Full sun or partial shade.*

Compost: *Use a general-purpose compost with a 60/40 mix of organic matter to grit.*

Feed: *Apply a balanced feed from spring until fall.*

Water: *Keep the compost well watered all year round; they like plenty of water and hate to dry out.*

Pests and diseases: *May suffer attacks from aphids and mildew.*

Goat Willow (*Salix caprea*).

AZALEA

These semi-evergreen and evergreen flowering shrubs are grown for their late spring to early summer flowers and glossy green foliage. Satsuki Azaleas are highly prized in Japan, and come in a variety of flower colors, including some bicolors. The flowers are very large and may completely obscure their branches and foliage. Some growers disbud areas of the tree to show off the flowers against the foliage.

Species and varieties used:
Rhododendron lateritium (*Satsuki Azalea, syn.* Rhododendron indicum), Rhododendron obtusum (*Kurume Azalea syn.* Rhododendron kiusianum), Rhododendron impeditum.
Bonsai styles: Informally styled specimens.

Satsuki Azalea
Hardiness: Hardy from 32°F to around 86°F.
Position: Partial shade.
Compost: Use acidic compost with a 70/30 mix of organic matter to grit.
Feed: Use a mild balanced feed from spring until flowering, then a low-nitrogen fed until fall. Check the feed is suitable for acid-loving plants.
Water: Water frequently in the growing season, keep moist in fall and winter, and do not allow to dry out.
Pests and diseases: Aphids and scale insects.

Kurume Azalea
Famous for the Kyushu hybrids.
Hardiness: Hardy from 32°F to 86°F. They need protection from frosts.
Position: Partial shade.
Compost: Acidic soil (Kanuma) with a 60/40 mix of organic matter to grit. Or try 50% Kanuma, 30% soil-less compost, 20% grit.
Feed: Use a mild balanced feed from spring until flowering, then a low-nitrogen feed until fall. Check the feed is suitable for acid-loving plants.
Water: Water these Azaleas frequently in the summer months, keep moist in spring and fall, and just moist over winter.
Pests and diseases: Aphids, scale insects, and vine weevils can be a problem for these plants.

A Satsuki Azalea in the Informal Upright style

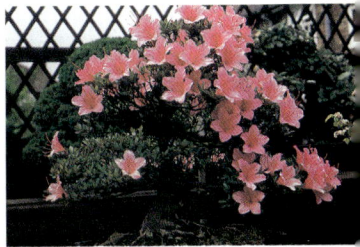

A beautiful Satsuki Azalea in full flower.

CEDAR (*Cedrus*)

These large coniferous evergreen trees originate from the Western Himalayas and the Mediterranean. Their branches have short spurts of foliage that weep at the tips. Mature specimens have an open habit with flat pads of foliage. There are lots of trees with Cedar as part of their common names—like Western Red Cedar (Thuja plicata)—*but these are not true Cedars.*

Species and varieties used: Cedrus atlantica *(Atlas Cedar)*, Cedrus atlantica 'Glauca' *(Blue Atlas Cedar)*, Cedrus brevifolia *(Cyprus Cedar)*, Cedrus deodara *(Deodar Cedar)*, and Cedrus libani *(Cedar of Lebanon)*.

Bonsai styles: *Formal and Informal Upright styles, Windswept, and Literati.*

Hardiness: *From 23°F to around 90°F.*

Position: *Full sun, and partial shade in summer.*

Compost: *Use an equal mix of Akadama (general-purpose bonsai compost) and Kureyu (bonsai compost for conifers), with a 60/40 mix of grit to organic matter.*

Feed: *Start with a nitrogen-rich feed in spring, do not feed through summer, then resume with a low-nitrogen feed in late summer.*

Water: *Keep on the dry side. Water frequently in summer, keep moist in spring and fall, and just moist in the winter months.*

Pests and diseases: *Aphids may be a problem.*

Atlas Cedar (*Cedrus atlantica*).

around 90°F.

Position: *Place in full sun or partial shade. Protect from direct sun in very hot weather in summer.*

Compost: *Use a general-purpose compost with a 60/40 mix of organic matter to grit.*

Feed: *Apply a balanced general-purpose fertilizer through the spring and summer, then a nitrogen-free fertilizer during the fall months.*

Water: *Water well in the growing season (summer). Keep very moist in spring and fall, and just moist through winter.*

Pests and diseases: *Cryptomeria may suffer attacks from scale insects, mealy bug, red spider mites, mildew, and gray mold. It is important to remove the dead foliage that collects at the center of the plant to allow air, light, and water into the canopy.*

CRYPTOMERIA

Often called Japanese Cedar, this is not a true member of the Cedar family. It originates in Japan, where specimens up to 200 ft. high can be seen growing on mountainsides. Consequently, the Japanese think of it as their answer to the Californian Redwood. It has interesting, peeling stringy bark and foliage that turns a reddish brown in winter.

Species and varieties used: *Bonsai growers use* Cryptomeria japonica *and* Cryptomeria japonica *'Yatsubusa'.*

Bonsai styles: *Upright styles with horizontal or drooping branches. Sometimes also used in group plantings.*

Hardiness: *Cryptomeria is hardy from 23°F to*

A group planting of
Hinoki Cypresses.

FALSE CYPRESS
(*Chamaecyparis*)

*These are conical evergreen
conifers from Thailand,
Japan, and North America.
They bear male and female
cones in spring and fall
respectively.*

Species and varieties used:
Chamaecyparis obtusa
(*Hinoki Cypress), and*
Chamaecyparis obtusa
'Nana' and 'Nana Gracilis'
*which are dwarf versions of
the Hinoki Cypress.*
Chamaecyparis pisifera
(Sawara Cypress),
Chamaecyparis pisifera
'Boulevard', *and*
Chamaecypars pisifera
'Squarrosa' *are also used
for bonsai.*
Bonsai styles: *Single
Informal and Formal
Upright styles, and Literati.
Also group plantings.*
Hardiness: *Hardy from
19ºF to 90ºF. Protect from
strong winds.*
Position: *Partial shade.*
Compost: *General-purpose
compost with a 60/40 mix
of organic matter to grit.*
Feed: *Use half-strength,
balanced general-purpose
feed from spring to fall.
Apply one nitrogen-free
feed in the late fall.*
Water: *Water well in spring
and summer, and keep
moist at all other times.
Don't allow to get dry.*
Pests and diseases: *Red
spider mite may be a
problem on False Cypress.*

FIG (*Ficus*)

These are mainly evergreen, tender, small to large trees from the moist tropical and subtropical forests. The species and varieties that are usually used for bonsai are closer to the figs often found as houseplants, and their jungle relatives, than the edible fig.

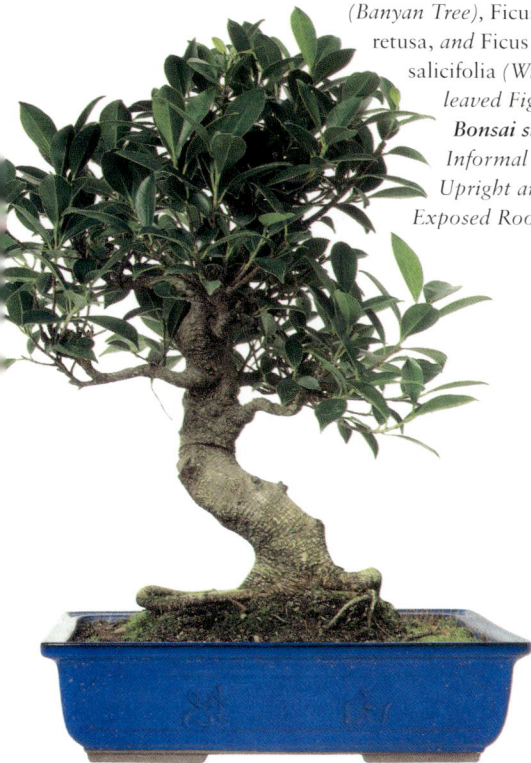

Species and varieties used:
Ficus benjamina (*Weeping Fig*), Ficus microphylla (*Banyan Tree*), Ficus retusa, *and* Ficus salicifolia (*Willow-leaved Fig*).

Bonsai styles:
Informal Upright and Exposed Root.

Hardiness: *These plants are tender—provide a minimum temperature of 59°F to around 98°F. They need high humidity and a stable temperature.*

Position: *Place in partial shade indoors, or outdoors in hot climates.*

Compost: *Use a general-purpose compost with a 60/40 mix of organic matter to grit.*

Feed: *Use a balanced general-purpose fertilizer from spring to fall and reduce to half strength through winter.*

Water: *Water well in spring and summer and mist the foliage regularly. Keep moist at all other times.*

Pests and diseases: *Figs may suffer attacks from scale insects.*

Ficus retusa (Indian Laurel Fig), also known as *Ficus microcarpa.*

FIR (*Abies*)

There are approximately 50 species of these evergreen conifers spread throughout Europe, Africa, North America, and Asia's mountainous regions. They have glossy flattened foliage which often has a silvery white line on the underside. Firs produce male and female cones. The pendent male cones are green at first and change to a purplish brown color when mature. The female cones appear on the upper branches of the tree in late spring and early summer and are purple to blue in color and upright. These plants are used as Christmas trees.

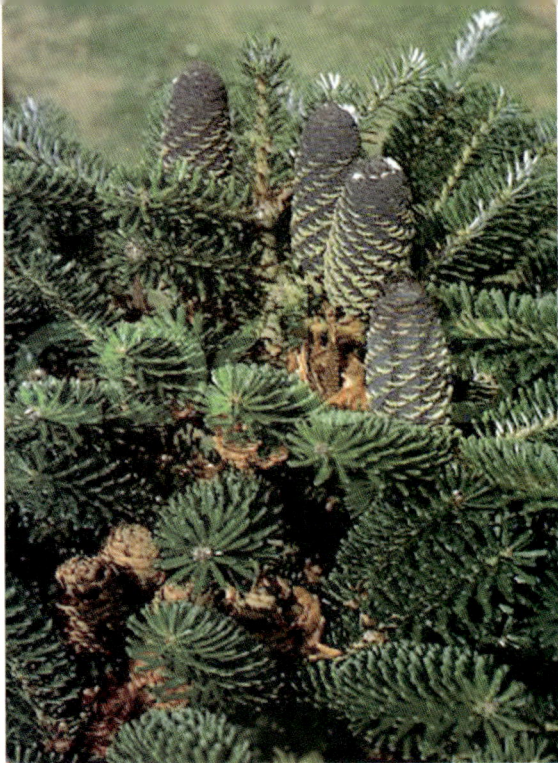

Korean Fir (*Abies koreana*).

Species and varieties used: Abies firma (*Japanese Fir*), Abies koreana (*Korean Fir*), and Abies sachalinensis (*Sakhalin Fir*) are often used for bonsai.

Bonsai styles: Formal and Informal Upright styles are popular. Also, Literati and small group plantings may be made from Firs.

Hardiness: These plants are hardy from 23°F to around 86°F.

Position: Partial shade.

Compost: General-purpose compost with a 60/40 mix of organic matter to grit.

Feed: Apply a balanced general-purpose feed from the spring to the fall.

Water: Water Firs well in the spring and summer months and mist the foliage regularly. Keep moist at all other times.

Pests and diseases: Aphids and scale insects can cause problems.

FIRETHORN (*Pyracantha*)

These are spiny, evergreen shrubs found growing wild in the scrub and woodland of Southern Europe, South West Asia, the Himalayas, China, and Taiwan. White flowers are produced in spring, followed by an abundance of either yellow, orange, or red berries. They have small leaves, sharp spines, and a vigorous growth habit.

Species and varieties used: Pyracantha angustifolia, Pyracantha 'Orange Charmer', Pyracantha 'Darts Red', and Pyracantha 'Soleil d'Or'.

Bonsai styles: *Informal Upright styles such as Horizontal and Semi-cascade. Their trunks thicken relatively slowly and are often trained over rocks at the base to give the plants the appearance of extra strength.*

Hardiness: *The Western species mentioned above are quite hardy, withstanding temperatures of 28°F to around 98°F. There are some tender species from the Philippines that will not survive below 41°F and ideally should be grown in a climate of around 54–68°F.*

Position: *Full sun or partial shade.*

Compost: *Use a general-purpose compost with a 60/40 mix of organic matter to grit.*

Feed: *Apply a balanced general-purpose feed in the spring and summer months, and a low-nitrogen feed through the fall.*

Water: *Pyracantha are thirsty plants. Keep them moist all year round and increase watering in the spring and summer.*

Pests and diseases: *Aphids, scale insects, red spider mites, and fireblight may be a problem.*

Firethorn in full bloom

IVY (*Hedera*)

Ivies can be found in many parts of the world, from North Africa to the Azores, the Canary Islands, and across Europe to the Himalayas, as well as in China, Korea, and Japan. Ivies are generally known as trailing or climbing plants which will cling to walls, fences, and trees, but their woody stems can be trained into successful bonsai.

Species and varieties used: Predominantly forms of Hedera helix, *which has a wealth of different leaf shapes and colors.*

Bonsai styles: Informal and Exposed Root styles.

Hardiness: Hardy from 23°F to around 86°F.

Position: Grow outside in full sun or partial shade. Ivies can also be grown indoors in partial shade.

Compost: Use a general-purpose compost with a 50/50 mix of organic matter to grit. They are not fussy and will grow in almost any soil.

Feed: Apply a balanced general-purpose fertilizer in the growing period.

Water: These plants will tolerate drought, so it is not essential to keep plants any more than moist year round. In very hot weather they tend to weep water from their leaves as a way of cooling themselves.

Pests and diseases: Ivies can suffer attacks from aphids and scale insects.

Two different styles of Ivy bonsai (*Hedera helix*).

JUNIPER
(*Juniperus*)

Junipers cover a wide range of shrubs and trees, from low-growing, spreading forms to tall forest trees which live on rocky hillsides and in dry forests all around the Northern hemisphere. Their foliage can be very sharp and is an irritant to most people's skin, bringing out a rash especially in sunny weather. These plants are unusual in that they have two types of foliage on the same plant. Juvenile foliage is spiky and needle-like, while the mature foliage is flat, scale-like, and overlaps. The trees produce male and female cones on separate trees. Male cones tend to be yellow and round or oval in shape, whereas the female cones are more like berries and are held on the tree for two or three years. Junipers are commonly used for bonsai.

Species and varieties used: There are a vast number of Junipers in cultivation, but

Chinese Juniper (*Juniperus chinensis*).

the ones with compact, fine foliage work best as bonsai. They range in color from steely blue-gray to light green and gold. Some examples are Juniperus californica (*Californian Juniper*), Juniperus chinensis (*Chinese Juniper*), Juniperus chinensis 'Sargentii' (*Sargent's Juniper*), Juniperus communis (*Common Juniper*), Juniperus conferta (*Shore Juniper*), Juniperus recurva (*Himalayan Weeping Juniper*), Juniperus rigida (*Needle Juniper*), Juniperus sabina (*Savin Juniper*), Juniperus virginiana (*Pencil Cedar*), Juniperus x media 'Blaauw', Juniperus x media 'Pfitzeriana', Juniperus x media 'San Jose', and Juniperus squamata (*Flaky Juniper*).
Bonsai styles: Many styles, both Informal and Formal,

Juniperus chinensis 'Sargentii' (Sargent's Juniper) grown in the Informal Upright style.

---

often including driftwood.

Sargent's Juniper

(Juniperus chinensis *'Sargentii' syn* Juniperus x media *'Shimpaku'*).

Hardiness: *Hardy from 14°F to 86°F. Cold weather can turn the foliage bronze.*

Position: *Full sun or light shade outdoors. The foliage takes on a better color in shade but the growth is more compact in sun.*

Compost: *General-purpose compost with a 60/40 mix of grit to organic matter.*

Feed: *Use a balanced general-purpose feed at half strength from spring to fall.*

Water: *Water well in spring and summer and keep moist in fall and winter.*

Pests and diseases: *Scale insects can be a problem.*

Needle Juniper

Juniperus rigida *has flaky bark which can be brushed off gently to reveal orange bark underneath.*

Hardiness: *Hardy from 23°F to 90°F. Foliage can turn bronze in cold weather. Protect from cold winds.*

Position: *Full sun outdoors.*

Compost: *General-purpose compost with a 60/40 mix of grit to organic matter.*

Feed: *Balanced general-purpose feed at half strength in spring and summer. Give nitrogen-free feeds in fall.*

Water: *Water well in summer but do not waterlog. Water less in spring and fall and keep just moist over winter.*

Pests and diseases: *Scale insects, red spider mites, and caterpillars.*

Meyer's Juniper

Juniperus squamata 'Meyerii'.

Hardiness: *Hardy from 14°F to 86°F. Protect from cold winds.*

Position: *Full sun.*

Compost: *General-purpose compost with a 60/40 mix of grit to organic matter.*

Feed: *Use a balanced general-purpose feed in spring and summer and a nitrogen-free feed in fall.*

Water: *Water well in spring and summer. Reduce in fall and keep just moist in winter. Mist with cold water all year round.*

Pests and diseases: *Red spider mites, scale insects, caterpillars, and fungal infections if congested.*

Needle Juniper (*Juniperus rigida*) with driftwood.

PINE (*Pinus*)

These upright trees are found from the Arctic Circle to Central America, Europe, North Africa, and South East Asia. Their habitat in the Northern hemisphere is dry, mountain regions. Pines are evergreen conifers often with striking bark. Their foliage consists of needles that are held in groups, usually of two or five. Trees produce yellow male catkins at the base of shoots in the spring; the female cones take two to three years to ripen before they are dropped from the branches. Pines are often used in bonsai.

Species and varieties used: Pinus densiflora *(Red Pine)*, Pinus parviflora *(White Pine), and* Pinus thunbergii *(Black Pine) are commonly used, as are* Pinus sylvestris *(Scots Pine) and its dwarf forms 'Nana', Beuvronensis' and 'Watererii'.*

Bonsai styles: *Many styles, both Informal, Formal, and Literati.*

Red Pine

Hardiness: *Hardy from 23°F to 90°F. They need a period of cold weather to harden the foliage and shut them down through winter.*
Position: *Full sun.*
Compost: *Good drainage is essential. Use a general-*purpose compost but allow a 70/30 mix of grit to organic matter.

Feed: *Use a weak solution of balanced general-purpose feed from spring until late summer. Change to a low-nitrogen feed until the end of fall. Feed developing trees more frequently than established specimens.*

Water: *Keep the soil moist but try not to let it remain saturated for long. Water most in spring, then reduce water levels through summer to winter.*

Pests and diseases: *Woolly aphids and mealy bugs love* to feed on the rich sap of the shoots and needles.

White Pine

This has a delicate color with leaves that are bluish green above and blue-white underneath. It is sometimes called Pinus pentaphylla. *It has smooth bark and is often grafted onto Black Pine to benefit from its fissured bark.*

Hardiness: *Hardy from 23°F to 90°F. Protect from long periods with temperatures below 23°F.*

White Pine (*Pinus parviflora* 'Himekomatsu').

Position: Full sun to partial shade. The foliage will obtain a better color and shorter needles in full sun. Not suitable indoors.

Compost: General-purpose compost with a 70/30 mix of grit to organic matter.

Feed: Use a weak solution of a balanced general-purpose feed through spring and summer, and a nitrogen-free feed in fall and early winter.

Water: Water well in spring and summer but do not waterlog. Water less in fall and keep just moist in winter. Protect the tree from excess rain.

Pests and diseases: Aphids, scale insect, and root aphids.

Black Pine

This plant has craggy bark and shiny dark needles.

Hardiness: Hardy from 14°F to 86°F. Needs a period of cold to induce dormancy, but protect during long periods of freezing weather.

Position: Full sun.

Compost: General-purpose compost with high drainage, such as an 80/20 mix of grit to organic matter. It is possible to grow Black Pines in almost 100% grit, but keep a check on moisture levels.

Feed: Use a balanced general-purpose feed in spring and summer and a low-nitrogen feed through the fall and early winter.

Water: Likes to be kept on the dry side. Only water when the soil begins to look dry. This will be far less frequently than with most bonsai and even less frequently in winter.

Pests and diseases: Woolly aphids and mealy bugs like to feed on the rich sap of the shoots and needles.

Black Pine (*Pinus thunbergii*).

SPRUCE (*Picea*)

There are 30 to 40 species of these evergreen conifers which can be found in cool temperate areas of the Northern hemisphere. They have needle-like leaves that grow singly around their shoots and naturally have whorl-like foliage. Female cones are produced on the ends of the main and side shoots, and are upright when flowering, then later hang downward. They ripen from green or red to purple-brown. Male cones are yellow or red-purple and appear in spring on the previous year's growth.

Species and varieties used:
Picea abies (*Common or Norway Spruce*), Picea glauca (*White Spruce*), Picea glauca albertiana 'Conica', Picea glehnii (*Sakhalin Spruce*), Picea jezoensis (*Ezo Spruce*), and Picea jezoensis hondoensis (*Hondo Spruce*).
Bonsai styles: *Upright styles, Formal and Informal, sometimes in*

A group of Ezo Spruce (*Picea jezoensis*).

groups, and possibly including driftwood. They are often grown on rocks.
Hardiness: *Hardy from 5°F to around 81°F. Very hardy but must have near-freezing weather over winter in order to remain healthy. In warmer areas, keep the tree in the shadiest part of your garden or yard area over winter.*
Position: *Full sun or partial shade.*
Compost: *General-purpose*

compost with a 70/30 mix of organic matter to grit.
Feed: *Use a balanced general-purpose feed from spring to summer and a nitrogen-free feed until fall.*
Water: *Keep these plants moist all year round but don't allow them to become waterlogged. Reduce amounts in winter.*
Pests and diseases: *Spruce may suffer attacks from aphids, red spider mites, galls, and rust.*

INDEX

CREDITS